CHARLES RENNIE MACKINTOSH

JOHN MCKE BAXTER

Colin Baxter Photography, Grantown-on-Spey, Scotland

CHARLES RENNIE MACKINTOSH

Charles Rennie Mackintosh, born in 1868, was Scotland's last great Victorian designer. Over a century later, his imagery stands out for its lasting freshness, making it still instantly memorable today. The interplay of nature and geometry, a central theme all his life, is reflected in the lattice chair-back (opposite), up which grows a stencilled rose.

Aiming to become an architect, Mackintosh joined a well-known practice in Glasgow after his teenage apprenticeship. Here he later became a partner on the strength of his designing a new Art School for the city when he was thirty; but by the time he was forty it was over. Instead of being at the centre of a prosperous architectural machine, he was falling off the edge of respectable life.

Circumstances – his mercurial artistic personality, his fin-de-siècle designs having fallen out of fashion as quickly as they had become the rage, and a drying-up of architectural work – were conspiring to extinguish any possible professional career. His brief international reputation evaporated and Mackintosh was now lost. With Margaret, his artist wife, he packed his bags in 1914 and lived in exile, almost penniless, until his death in 1928.

THE INTERIOR

Mackintosh's genius lay in his interiors; not so much in individual items, but in the ensembles of often exquisite forms arranged with great spatial skill. Yet everywhere the fragments can stand alone: the graphic inventiveness in this glazed rose on a bookcase door panel; the geometric satisfaction in the subdivision of the 100 glass squares of the hallway window; the fusion of nature and geometry in the tulip head cut from the metal cube light.

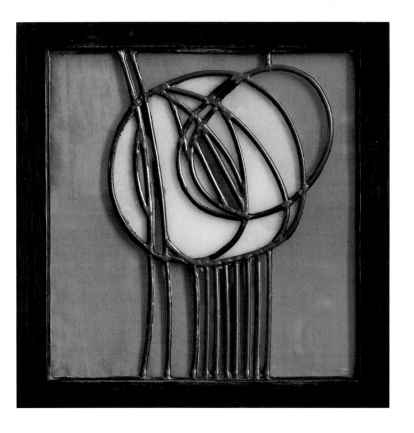

QUEEN'S CROSS CHURCH, PULPIT DETAIL

THE CHURCH

Mackintosh's only church appears at first glance traditional in form and material. But looking closer, you see much more in its slightly asymmetric spaces and on its surfaces which are loaded with symbolic meanings. The oak pulpit, with its great halo behind the minister's head, has an enveloping bird swooping on grain, probably indicating the parable of the sower. While overhead soars an upturned hull, held together by a great, riveted steel tie beam.

GLASGOW SCHOOL OF ART

Mackintosh's architectural career is encompassed by this building, which his genius raised beyond the modest provincial School of Art it might have been. It was his first and last great building. Once more, the overall shape is straightforwardly traditional, but between huge north-facing studio windows he fits an asymmetric castle-like entrance. Only half complete when opened in 1899, the section to the right of the entrance is a decade newer.

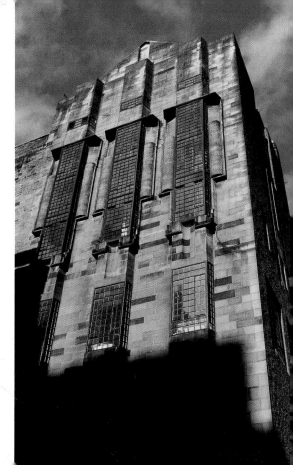

THE ART SCHOOL

When he came to build the second half a decade later, Mackintosh didn't alter the overall form – it is virtually impossible to see the join.

But one space, the library (left), was completely redesigned; and its external west wall became different from the traditional appearance originally proposed. Internally it is an extraordinary forest, its balcony and ceiling standing clear of the soaring windows.

GLASGOW SCHOOL OF ART, CLOCK

THE MACKINTOSH HOUSE

Like so much of his small output as architect and designer, Mackintosh's own house was demolished, though has since been meticulously recreated. Mackintosh, in his few years as a Glasgow interior designer, was forever reusing elements. In each new place, and particularly in his own house, the ensembles – whether elegant white or mysterious dark furniture, lamps or wall stencilling – come together to create new spaces.

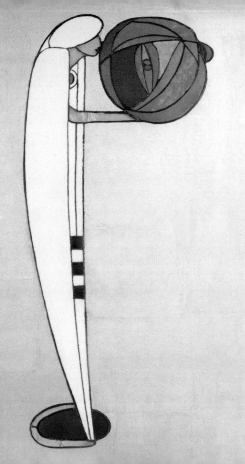

THEIR HOME

In 1906, the Mackintoshes formed this home for themselves in the shell of a Victorian end-of-terrace. The focal point was the white drawing room and studio, a most unexpected and calm, L-shaped space. Its furniture, which appears out of the white mist, was often of elegantly simple shape and exquisitely ornamented in detail – as seen in this lady with the rose, inlaid in the silvered door of a little cabinet.

THE MACKINTOSH BEDROOM

The white bedroom suite – large, cubic, four-poster bed
and free-standing mirror – was designed by Mackintosh
for his marriage to Margaret in 1900; the extremely elegant
metal panel above the fireplace by Margaret herself. It was
an extraordinary, outrageous room to land amongst the
overwhelming clutter of a late-Victorian domestic city.

WINDYHILL

In his first house (at Kilmacolm around 1900) Mackintosh interpreted traditional domestic architectural forms. While the undecorated, simple volumes appear rather masculine and dour outside, there is a very different, feminine interior, including the rose decoration (opposite) in the charming white bedroom.

HOUSE FOR AN ART LOVER

This large country house, recently built in a Glasgow park,
is based on Mackintosh sketches entered for a magazine's
'ideas competition' in 1901. In the 1990s, craftsmen lovingly
enriched the surfaces of its overscaled spaces like the
dining room (opposite), in tasteful homage to the master
of a century ago.

THE HILL HOUSE

In 1902 Mackintosh was commissioned for a second suburban house, The Hill House in Helensburgh. This is his domestic masterpiece, where his confidence as an architect and interior designer are finally matched.

Traditional Baronial memories outside belie a very different interior. On entering, we are in a darkly lined hall on two levels. It is almost a forest clearing through which the stair winds up, past cubical, hanging light-frames.

THE HILL HOUSE

After entering the hard, masonry shell and climbing through the dark, wooded hall and stair, you reach the softest, light, white spaces at the building's heart: the main bedroom.

This L-shaped room, with its vaulted bed-space, is formed with a precise geometry though it appears fantastic and exotic. The walls lined with flowing roses and the handleless wardrobe door in lacquered cream (left), reiterate Mackintosh's constant linking of geometry and nature.

THE HILL HOUSE, MAIN BEDROOM

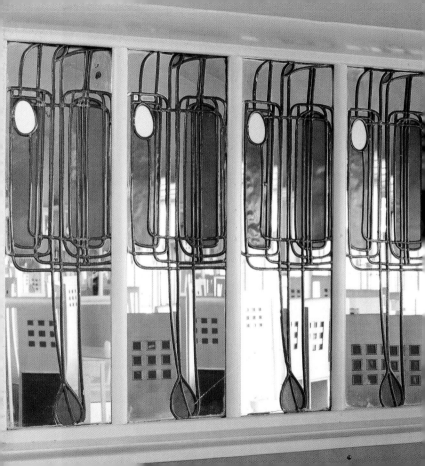

THE WILLOW TEA ROOMS

Mackintosh's last and most remarkable tea-room, fitted out in 1903, centred on the Room De Luxe on the first floor. This vaulted space is circled by a deep band at eye height, part mirror part window. To the street, glazed panes each have a mirrored heart (right); to the sides mirrored panes are leaded with purple and pink (left). Within this dissolving visual complexity, tall silver chairs with translucent pink squares are once again in use today.

SCOTLAND STREET SCHOOL

The larger of the two schools designed by Mackintosh, Scotland Street (1903-6) is once again conventionally shaped. But here the architect forms two great stair towers on the front, flanking the hall and two further storeys of classrooms. Inside, these are exciting, tall semi-cylinders of space. Glasgow's red sandstone and slate roofs are transformed by Mackintosh into extraordinary, daring columns of masonry and glass under their conical hats.

FLOWERS

Mackintosh drew flowers all his life, but was particularly prolific in the year after he left Glasgow, when he produced little else. Breaking completely with architecture in 1914, he became absorbed in a project of botanical studies in pencil and watercolour. Not only technically accurate observational drawings, they are elegant pictorial compositions of great beauty. This is a rare later example drawn in the Sussex countryside in 1919.

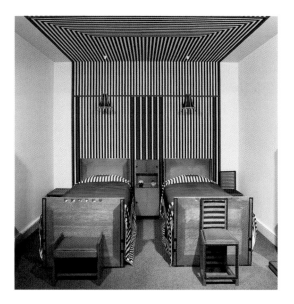

THE WARTIME DESIGNER

In London (1915-23), Mackintosh's meagre output was largely decorative, with textile designs (left) and one interior. This Northampton guest room, with its dramatic stripes set off by simple oak furniture, was a powerful design, far removed from anything he had done before.

THE FRENCH PAINTER

After unproductive years in London, and in financial difficulty, the Mackintoshes left Britain, reaching French Catalonia early in 1924. Having left architecture and design for a second and now final time, he focused again on his watercolours. Drained of figures, drained entirely of his earlier symbolism, they move towards a new almost mute, impersonal vision. However, there was little interest in exhibiting them in London, whence Mackintosh returned in 1927, dying of cancer aged sixty, less than a year later.

With his astonishing range of works – jewellery, graphics, wall decoration and all kinds of domestic objects – he resembled those Art Nouveau designers famed for work produced within a very few years a century ago. With his unique interiors and his few buildings from the same years, he never fitted alongside architects of his generation who could work very differently after one, even two, world wars. Distinct from either of these groups, Mackintosh's personal path produced the exquisite portfolio of flowers from 1914-5 and finally, in 1924-7, his series of crystalline French landscapes.

It was a quite unique career.

AN ARTIST'S COUNTRY COTTAGE

Paperback edition published in 2009
First published in Great Britain in 2002 by Colin Baxter Photography Ltd,
Grantown-on-Spey, PH26 3NA, Scotland.
www.colinbaxter.co.uk

Text by John McKean, Copyright © Colin Baxter Photography Ltd, 2009
All photography copyright © Colin Baxter 2009 except: T & R Annan & Sons Ltd: 3;
Glasgow Museums: Art Gallery and Museums: 31; Glasgow School of Art: 30; Hunterian Art Gallery,
University of Glasgow, Mackintosh Collection: 27, 28. The publishers would like to thank the following
for their kind permission to reproduce images in this book: T & R Annan & Sons Ltd; The CRM Society;
Mrs Fisher; Glasgow Museums: Art Gallery & Museums, Kelvingrove; Glasgow School of Art; Hendersons
the Jewellers; The Hill House, The National Trust for Scotland; The House For An Art Lover; Hunterian
Art Gallery, University of Glasgow, Mackintosh Collection; Scotland Street School; Hans Van Kessel.

A CIP catalogue record for this book is available from the British Library.

ISBN 978-1-84107-443-6   *Colin Baxter Gift Book Series*   Printed in China

Front cover photograph: *Stained Glass Detail from the Rose Boudoir.*
Page one photograph: *Drawing Room Lamp & Wall Stencils, The Hill House, Helensburgh.*
Back cover photograph: *Bedroom Fireplace Detail, The Hill House, Helensburgh.*